LITTLE BLUE BOOK NO. 30
Edited by E. Haldeman-Julius

What Life Means to Me

Jack London

HALDEMAN-JULIUS COMPANY
GIRARD, KANSAS

What Life Means To Me

By Jack London

I was born into the working class. I early discovered enthusiasm, ambition, and ideals; and to satisfy these became the problem of my childlife. My environment was crude and rough and raw. I had no outlook, but an uplook rather. My place in society was at the bottom. Here life offered nothing but sordidness and wretchedness, both of the flesh and the spirit; for here flesh and spirit were alike starved and tormented.

Above me towered the colossal edifice of society, and to my mind the only way out was up. Into this edifice I early resolved to climb. Up above, men wore black clothes and boiled shirts, and women dressed in beautiful gowns. Also, there were good things to eat, and there was plenty to eat. This much for the flesh. Then there were the things of the spirit. Up above me, I knew, were unselfishness of the spirit, clean and noble thinking, keen intellectual living. I knew all this because I read

"Seaside Library" novels, in which, with the exception of the villains and adventuresses, all men and women thought beautiful thoughts, spoke a beautiful tongue, and performed glorious deeds. In short, as I accepted the rising of the sun, I accepted that up above me was all that was fine and noble and gracious, all that gave decency and dignity to life, all that made life worth living and that remunerated one for his travail and misery.

But it is not particularly easy for one to climb up out of the working class—especially if he is handicapped by the possession of ideals and illusions. I lived on a ranch in California, and I was hard put to find the ladder whereby to climb. I early inquired the rate of interest on invested money, and worried my child's brain into an understanding of the virtues and excellences of that remarkable invention of man, compound interest. Further, I ascertained the current rates of wages for workers of all ages, and the cost of living. From all these data I concluded that if I began immediately and worked and saved until I was fifty years of age, I could then stop working and enter into participation in a fair portion of the delights and goodnesses that would then be open to me higher up in society. Of course, I resolutely determined not to marry, while I quite forgot to consider at all that great rock of disaster in the working class world—sickness.

But the life that was in me demanded more than a meager existence of scraping and scrimping. Also, at ten years of age, I became a newsboy on the streets of a city, and found myself with a changed uplook. All about me were still the same sordidness and wretchedness, and up above me was still the same paradise waiting to be gained; but the ladder whereby to climb was a different one. It was now the ladder of business. Why save my earnings and invest in government bonds, when by buying two newspapers for five cents, with a turn of the wrist I could sell them for ten cents and double my capital? The business ladder was the ladder for me, and I had a vision of myself becoming a baldheaded and successful merchant prince. . . .

[The author became the owner of an oyster-boat, and thereby a capitalist; but was ruined by the burning of his boat.]

From then on I was mercilessly exploited by other capitalists. I had the muscle, and they made money out of it while I made but a very indifferent living out of it. I was a sailor before the mast, a longshoreman, a roustabout; I worked in canneries, and factories, and laundries; I mowed lawns, and cleaned carpets, and washed windows. And I never got the full product of my toil. I looked at the daughter of the cannery owner, in her carriage, and knew that it was my muscle, in part, that helped drag along that carriage on its rubber tires. I looked at the son of the factory owner, going to college, and knew that it was my muscle that helped, in part, to pay for the wine and good-fellowship he enjoyed.

But I did not resent this. It was all in the game. They were the strong. Very well, I was strong. I would carve my way to a place among them, and make money out of the muscles of other men. I was not afraid of work. I loved hard work. I would pitch in and work harder than ever and eventually become a pillar of society.

And just then, as luck would have it, I found an employer that was of the same mind. I was willing to work, and he was more than willing that I should work. I thought I was learning a trade. In reality, I had displaced two men. I thought he was making an electrician out of me; as a matter of fact, he was making $50 per month out of me. The two men I had displaced had received $40 each per month; I was doing the work of both for $30 per month.

This employer worked me nearly to death. A man may love oysters, but too many oysters will disincline him toward that particular diet. And so with me. Too much work sickened me. I did not wish ever to see work again. I fled from work. I became a tramp, begging my way from door to door, wandering over the United States, and sweating bloody sweats in slums and prisons.

I had been born in the working class, and I was now, at the age of eighteen, beneath the point at which I had started. I was down in the cellar of society, down in the subterranean depths of misery about which it is neither nice nor proper to speak. I was in the pit, the abyss, the human cesspool, the shambles and the charnel house of our civilization. This is the part of the edifice of society that society chooses to ignore. Lack of space compels me here to ignore it, and I shall say only that the things I there saw gave me a terrible scare.

[The author reflected, and decided that it

was better to sell brains than muscle.] Then began a frantic pursuit of knowledge. I returned to California and opened the books. While thus equipping myself to become a brain merchant, it was inevitable that I should delve into sociology. There I found, in a certain class of books, scientifically formulated, the simple sociological concepts I had already worked out for myself. Other and greater minds, before I was born, had worked out all that I had thought, and a vast deal more. I discovered that I was a Socialist.

The Socialists were revolutionists, inasmuch as they struggled to overthrow the society of the present, and out of the material to build the society of the future. I, too, was a Socialist, and a revolutionist. I joined the groups of working-class and intellectual revolutionists, and for the first time came into intelligent living. Here I found keen-flashing intellects and brilliant wits; for here I met strong and alert-brained, withal horny-handed, members of the working class; unfrocked preachers too wide in their Christianity for any congregation of Mammon-worshippers; professors broken on the wheel of university subservience to the ruling class and flung out because they were quick with knowledge which they strove to apply to the affairs of mankind.

Here I found, also, warm faith in the human, glowing idealism, sweetness of unselfishness, renunciation and martyrdom—all the splendid, stinging things of the spirit. Here life was clean, noble, and alive. Here life rehabilitated itself, became wonderful and glorious; and I was glad to be alive. I was in touch with great souls who exalted flesh and spirit over dollars and cents; and to whom the thin wails of the starved slum-child meant more than all the pomp and circumstance of commercial expansion and world-empire. All about me were nobleness of purpose and heroism of effort, and my days and nights were sunshine and starshine, all fire and dew, with before my eyes, ever burning and blazing, the Holy Grail, Christ's own Grail, the warm human, long suffering and maltreated, but to be rescued and saved at the last. . . .

As a brain merchant I was a success. Society opened its portals to me. I entered right in on the parlor floor, and my disillusionment proceeded rapidly. I sat down to dinner with the masters of society, and with the wives and daughters of the masters of society. The women were gowned beautifully, I admit; but to my naive surprise I discovered that they were of the same clay as all the rest of the women I had known down below in the cellar. "The colonel's lady and Judy O'Grady were sisters under their skins"—and gowns.

It was not this, however, so much as their materialism, that shocked me. It is true these beautifully gowned, beautiful women prattled sweet little ideals and dear little moralities; but in spite of their prattle the dominant key of the life they lived was materialistic. And they were so sentimentally selfish! They assisted in all kinds of sweet little charities, and informed one of the fact, while all the time the food they ate and the beautiful clothes they wore were bought out of dividends stained with the blood of child labor, and sweated labor, and of prostitution itself. When I mentioned such facts, expecting in my innocence that these sisters of Judy O'Grady would at once strip off their blood-dyed silks and jewels, they became excited and angry, and read me preachments about the lack of thrift, the drink, and the innate depravity that caused all the misery in society's cellar. When I mentioned

that I couldn't quite see that it was the lack
of thrift, the intemperance, and the depravity
of a half-starved child of six that made it
work twelve hours every night in a Southern
cotton mill, these sisters of Judy O'Grady attacked my private life and called me an "agi-
tator"—as though that, forsooth, settled the
argument.

Nor did I fare better with the masters themselves. I had expected to find men who were
clean, noble and alive, whose ideals were clean,
noble and alive. I went out amongst the men
who sat in the high places, the preachers, the
politicians, the business men, the professors,
and the editors. I ate meat with them, drank
wine with them, automobiled with them, and
studied them. It is true, I found many that
were clean and noble; but, with rare exceptions,
they were not alive. I do verily believe I
could count the exceptions on the fingers of
my two hands. Where they were not alive with
rottenness, quick with unclean life, they were
merely the unburied dead—clean and noble,
like well-preserved mummies, but not alive.
In this connection I may especially mention
the professors I met, the men who live up to
that decadent univerity ideal, "the passionless

pursuit of passionless intelligence."

I met men who invoked the name of the Prince of Peace in their diatribes against war, and who put rifles in the hands of Pinkertons with which to shoot down strikers in their own factories. I met men incoherent with indignation at the brutality of prize-fighting, and who, at the same time, were parties to the adulteration of food that killed each year more babies than even red-handed Herod had killed.

I discovered that I did not like to live on the parlor floor of society. Intellectually I was bored. Morally and spiritually I was sickened. I remembered my intellectuals and idealists, my unfrocked preachers, broken professors, and clean-minded, class-conscious workingmen. I remembered my days and nights of sunshine and starshine, where life was all a wild wonder, a spiritual paradise of unselfish adventure and ethical romance. And I saw before me, ever blazing and burning, the Holy Grail.

So I went back to the working class, in which I had been born and where I belonged. I care no longer to climb. This imposing edifice of society above my head holds no delight for me. It is the foundation of the edifice that interests me. There I am content to labor, crowbar in hand, shoulder to shoulder with intellectuals, idealists, and class-conscious workingmen, getting a solid pry now and again and setting the whole edifice rocking. Some day, when we get a few more hands and crowbars to work, we'll topple it over, along with all its rotten life and unburied dead, its monstrous selfishness and sodden materialism. Then we'll cleanse the cellar and build a new habitation for mankind, in which there will be no parlor floor, in which all the rooms will be bright and airy, and where the air that is breathed will be clean, noble and alive.

A THOUGHT.

Far better to have the front of one's face pushed in by the fist of an honest prize-fighter than to have the lining of one's stomach corroded by the embalmed beef of a dishonest manufacturer.—Jack London.

Dream of Debs

By Jack London

I awoke fully an hour before my customary time. This in itself was remarkable, and I lay very wide awake, pondering over it. Something was the matter, something was wrong— I knew not what. I was oppressed by a premonition of something terrible that had happened or was about to happen. But what was it? I strove to orientate myself. I remembered that at the time of the Great Earthquake of 1906 many claimed they awakened some moments before the first shock and that during those moments they experienced strange feelings of dread. Was San Francisco again to be visited by earthquake?

I lay for a full minute, numbly expectant, but there occurred no reeling of walls nor shock and grind of falling masonry. All was quiet. That was it! The silence! No wonder I had been perturbed. The hum of the great live city was strangely silent. The surface cars passed along my street at that time of day, on an average of one every three minutes; but in the ten succeeding minutes not a car passed. Perhaps it was a street railway strike, was my thought; or perhaps there had been an accident and the power was shut off. But no, the silence was too profound. I heard no jar and rattle of wagon-wheels, nor stamp of iron-shod hoofs straining up the steep cobble-stones.

Pressing the push-button beside my bed, I strove to hear the sound of the bell, though I knew it was impossible for the sound to rise three stories to me even if the bell did ring. It rang all right, for a few minutes later Brown entered with the tray and morning paper. Though his features were impassive as ever, I noted a startled, apprehensive light in his eyes. I noted, also, that there was no cream on the tray.

"The creamery did not deliver this morning," he explained; "nor did the baker."

I glanced again at the tray. There were no fresh French rolls—only slices of stale graham bread from yesterday, the most detestable of bread so far as I was concerned.

"Nothing was delivered this morning, sir." Brown started to explain apologetically; but I interrupted him.

"The paper?"

"Yes, sir, it was delivered, but it was the only thing, and it is the last time, too. There won't be any paper tomorrow. The paper says so. Can I send out and get you some condensed milk?"

I shook my head, accepted the coffee black, and spread open the paper. The headlines explained everything—explained too much, in fact, for the lengths of pessimism to which the journal went, were ridiculous. A general strike, it said, had been called all over the United States; and most foreboding anxieties were expressed concerning the provisioning of the great cities.

I read on hastily, skimming much and remembering much of the labor troubles in the past. For a generation the general strike had been the dream of organized labor, which dream had arisen originally in the mind of Debs, one of the great leaders of thirty years before. I recollected that in my young college-settlement days I had even written an article on the subject for one of the magazines and that I had entitled it, "The Dream of Debs." And I must confess that I had treated the idea very carefully and academically as a dream and nothing more. Time and the world had rolled on, Gompers was gone, the American Federation of Labor was gone, and gone was Debs with all his wild revolutionary ideas; but the dream had persisted, and here it was at last realized in fact. But I laughed, as I read, at the journal's gloomy outlook. I knew better. I had seen organized labor worsted in too many conflicts. It would be a matter only of days when the thing would be settled. This was a national strike, and it wouldn't take the government long to break it.

I threw the paper down and proceeded to dress. It would certainly be interesting to be out in the streets of San Francisco when not a wheel was turning and the whole city was taking an enforced vacation.

"I beg your pardon, sir," Brown said, as he handed me my cigar case, "but Mr. Harmmed has asked to see you before you go out."

"Send him in right away," I answered.

Harmmed was the butler. When he entered I could see he was laboring under controlled excitement. He came at once to the point.

"What shall I do, sir? There will be needed provisions, and the delivery drivers are on strike. And the electricity is shut off—I guess they're on strike, too."

"Are the shops open?" I asked.

"Only the small ones, sir. The retail clerks are out and the big ones can't open; but the owners and their families are running the little ones themselves."

"Then take the machine," I said, "and go the rounds and make your purchases. Buy plenty of everything you need or may need. Get a box of candles—no, get half a dozen boxes. And when you're done, tell Harrison to bring the machine around to the club for me—not later than eleven."

Harmmed shook his head gravely. "Mr. Harrison has struck along with the Chauffeurs' Union, and I don't know how to run the machine myself."

"Oh, ho, he has, has he?" I said. "Well, when next Mister Harrison happens around you tell him that he can look elsewhere for a position."

"Yes, sir."

"You don't happen to belong to a Butlers' Union, do you, Harmmed?"

"No, sir," was the answer. "And even if I did I'd not desert my employer in a crisis like this. No, sir, I would—"

"All right, thank you," I said. "Now you get ready to accompany me. I'll run the machine myself. and we'll lay in a stock of provisions to stand a siege."

It was a beautiful first of May, even as May days go. The sky was cloudless, there was no wind, and the air was warm—almost balmy. Many autos were out, but the owners were driving them themselves. The streets were crowded but quiet. The working class, dressed in its Sunday best, was out taking the air and observing the effects of the strike. It was all so unusual, and withal so peaceful, that I found myself enjoying it. My nerves were tingling with mild excitement. It was a sort of placid adventure. I passed Miss Chick-ering. She was at the helm of her little runabout. She swung around and came after me, catching me at the corner.

"Oh, Mr. Cerf!" she hailed. "Do you know where I can buy candles? I've been to a dozen shops, and they're all sold out. It's dreadfully awful, isn't it?"

But her sparkling eyes gave the lie to her words. Like the rest of us, she was enjoying it hugely. Quite an adventure it was, getting those candles. It was not until we went across the city and down into the working class quarter south of Market street that we found small corner groceries that had not yet sold out. Miss Chickering thought one box was sufficient but I persuaded her into taking four. My car was large, and I laid in a dozen boxes. There was no telling what delays might arise in the settlement of the strike. Also I filled the car with sacks of flour, baking powder, tinned goods, and all the ordinary necessaries of life suggested by Harmmed, who fussed around and clucked over the purchases like an anxious old hen.

The remarkable thing, that first day of the strike, was that no one really apprehended anything serious. The announcement of organized labor in the morning papers that it was prepared to stay out a month or three months was laughed at. And yet that very first day we might have guessed as much from the fact that the working class took practically no part in the great rush to buy provisions. Of course not. For weeks and months, craftily and secretly, the whole working class had been laying in private stocks of provisions. That was why we were permitted to go down and buy out the little groceries in the working class neighborhoods.

It was not until I arrived at the Club that afternoon that I began to feel the first alarm. Everything was in confusion. There were no olives for the cocktails, and the service was by hitches and jerks. Most of the men were angry, and all were worried. A babel of voices greeted me as I entered. General Folsom, nursing his capacious paunch in a window-seat in the smoking-room, was defending him-self against half a dozen excited gentlemen who were demanding that he do something.

"What can I do more than I have done?" he was saying. "There are no orders from Washington. If you gentlemen will get a wire through I'll do anything I am commanded to do. But I don't see what can be done. The first thing I did this morning, as soon as I learned of the strike, was to order in the troops from the Presidio—three thousand of them. They're guarding the banks, the mint, the postoffice, and all the public buildings. There is no disorder whatever. The strikers are keeping the peace perfectly. You can't expect me to shoot them down as they walk along the streets with wives and children all in their best bib and tucker."

"I'd like to know what's happening on Wall Street," I heard Jimmy Wombold say as I passed along. I could imagine his anxiety, for I knew that he was deep in the big Consolidated-Western deal.

"Say, Cerf," Atkinson bustled up to me, "is your machine running?"

"Yes," I answered, "but what's the matter with your own?"

"Broken down and the garages are all closed. And my wife's somewhere around Truckee, I think, stalled on the Overland. Can't get a wire to her for love or money. She should have arrived this evening. She may be starving. Lend me your machine.”

“Can’t get it across the bay,” Halsted spoke up. “The ferries aren’t running. But I tell you what you can do. There’s Rollinson—oh, Rollinson, come here a moment. Atkinson wants to get a machine across the bay. His wife is stuck on the Overland at Truckee. Can’t you bring the Lurlette across from Tiburon and carry the machine over for him?”

The “Lurlette” was a two-hundred-ton ocean-going schooner-yacht.

Rollinson shook his head. “You couldn’t get a longshoreman to load the machine on board, even if I could get the ‘Lurlette’ over, which I can’t, for the crew are members of the Coast Seamen’s Union, and they’re on strike along with the rest.”

“But my wife may be starving,” I could hear Atkinson wailing as I moved on.

At the other end of the smoking room I ran into a group of men bunched excitedly and angrily around Bertie Messener. And Bertie was stirring them up and prodding them in his cool, cynical way. Bertie didn’t care about the strike. He didn’t care much about anything. He was blase—at least in all the clean things of life; the nasty things had no attraction for him. He was worth twenty millions, all of it in safe investments, and he had never done a tap of productive work in his life—inherited it all from his father and two uncles. He had been everywhere, seen everything, and done everything but get married, and this last in the face of the grim and determined attack of a few hundred ambitious mammas. For years he had been the greatest catch, and as yet he had avoided being caught. He was disgracefully eligible. On top of his wealth, he was young and handsome, and, as I said before, clean. He was a great althlete, a young blond god that did everything perfectly and admirably with the solitary exception of matrimony. And he didn't care about anything, had no ambitions, no passions, no desire to do the very things he did so much better than other men.

"This is sedition!" one man in the group was crying. Another called it revolt and revolution, and another called it anarchy.

"I can't see it," Bertie said. "I have been out in the streets all morning. Perfect order reigns. I never saw a more law-abiding populace. There's no use calling it names. It's not any of these things. It's just what it claims to be, a general strike, and it's your turn to play, gentlemen."

"And we'll play all right!" cried Garfield, one of the traction millionaires. "We'll show this dirt where its place is—the beasts! Wait till the government takes a hand."

"But where is the government?" Bertie interposed. "It might as well be at the bottom of the sea so far as you're concerned. You don't know what's happening at Washington. You don't know whether you've got a government or not."

"Don't you worry about that!" Garfield blurted out.

"I assure you I'm not worrying," Bertie smiled languidly. "But it seems to me it's what you fellows are doing. Look in the glass, Garfield."

Garfield did not look, for had he looked, he would have seen a very excited gentleman with rumpled, iron-gray hair, a flushed face, mouth sullen and vindictive, and eyes wildly gleaming.

"It's not right, I tell you," little Hanover said; and from his tone I was sure that he had already said it a number of times.

"Now, that's going too far, Hanover," Bertie replied. "You fellows make me tired. You're all open-shop men. You've eroded my ear-drums with your endless gabble for the open-shop and the right of a man to work. You've harangued along those lines for years. Labor is doing nothing wrong in going out on this general strike. It is violating no law of God nor man. Don't you talk, Hanover. You've been ringing the changes too long on the God-given right to work . . . or not to work; you can't escape the corollary. It's a dirty little sordid scrap, that's all the whole thing is. You've got labor down and gouged it, and now labor's got you down and is gouging you, that's all, and you're squealing."

Every man in the group broke out in indig-nant denials that labor had ever been gouged.

"No, sir!" Garfield was shouting, "we've done the best for labor. Instead of gouging it, we've given it a chance to live. We've made work for it. Where would labor be if it hadn't been for us?"

"A whole lot better off," Bertie sneered. "You've got labor down and gouged it every

time you got a chance, and you went out of
your way to make chances."

"No! No!" were the cries.

"There was the teamsters' strike right here
in San Francisco," Bertie went on imperturbably. "The Employers' Association precipitated that strike. You know that. And
you know I know it, too, for I've sat in these
rooms and heard the inside talk and news of
the fight. First you precipitated the strike,
then you bought the Mayor and the Chief of
Police and broke the strike. A pretty spectacle, you philanthropists getting the teamsters
down and gouging them.

"Hold on, I'm not through with you. It's
only last year that the labor ticket of Colorado elected a Governor. He was never seated.
You know why. You know how your brother
philanthropists and capitalists of Colorado
worked it. It was a case of getting labor down
and gouging it. You kept the President of
the Southwestern Amalgamated Association
of Miners in a jail for three years on trumped-
up murder charges, and with him out of the
way you broke up the Association. That was
gouging labor; you'll admit. The third time
the graduated income tax was declared uncon-

stitutional was a gouge. So was the Eight-hour Bill you killed in the last Congress.

"And of all the unmitigated immoral gouges, your destruction of the closed-shop principle was the limit. You know how it was done. You bought our Farburg, the last president of the old American Federation of Labor. He was your creature—or the creature of all the trusts and employers' associations, which is the same thing. You precipitated the big Closed Shop Strike. Farburg betrayed that strike. You won, and the old American Federation of Labor crumpled to pieces. You fellows destroyed it, and by so doing undid yourselves; for right on top of it began the organization of the I. L. W.—the biggest and solidest organization of labor the United States has ever seen, and you are responsible for its existence and for the present general strike. You smashed all the old federations and drove labor in the I. L. W., and the I. L. W. called the general strike—still fighting for the closed shop. And then you have the effrontery to stand here face to face and tell me that you never got labor down and gouged it. Bah!"

This time there were no denials. Garfield

broke out in self-defense:

"We've done nothing we were not compelled to do, if we were to win."

"I'm not saying anything about that," Bertie answered. "What I am complaining about is your squealing now that you're getting a taste of your own medicine. How many strikes have you won by starving labor into submission? Well, labor's worked out a scheme whereby to starve you into submission. It wants the closed shop, and if it can get it by starving you, starve you shall."

"I notice that you have profited in the past by those very labor-gouges you mentioned," insinuated Brentwood, one of the wiliest and most astute of our corporation lawyers. "The receiver is as bad as the thief," he sneered. "You had no hand in the gouging, but you took your whack out of the gouge."

"That is quite beside the question, Brentwood," Bertie drawled. "You're as bad as Hanover, intruding the moral element. I haven't said that anything is right or wrong. It's all a rotten game, I know; and my sole kick is that you fellows are squealing now that you're down and labor's taking a gouge out of you. Of course I've taken the profits from the gouging, and, thanks to you, gentle-men, without having personally to do the dirty work. You did that for me—oh, believe me, not because I am more virtuous than you, but because my good father and his various brothers left me a lot of money with which to pay for the dirty work."

"If you mean to insinuate—" Brentwood began hotly.

"Hold on, don't get all ruffled up," Bertie interposed insolently. "There's no use in playing hypocrite in this thieves' den. The high and lofty is all right for the newspapers, boys' clubs and Sunday schools—that's part of the game; but for heaven's sake, don't let's play it on one another. You know, and you know I know, just what jobbery was done in the building trades strike last fall, who put up the money, who did the work, and who profited by it." (Brentwood flushed darkly.) "But we are all tarred with the same brush, and the best thing for us to do is to leave the morality out of it. Again I repeat, play the game, play it to the last finish, but for goodness' sake, don't squeal when you get hurt."

When I left the group Bertie was off on a

new tack tormenting them with the more serious aspects of the situation, pointing out the shortage of supplies that was already making itself felt, and asking them what they were going to do about it. A little later I met him in the cloak room, leaving, and gave him a lift home in my machine.

"It's a great stroke, this general strike," he said, as we bowled along through the crowded but orderly streets. "It's a smashing body-blow. Labor caught us napping and struck at our weakest place, the stomach. I'm going to get out of San Francisco, Cerf. Take my advice and get out, too. Head for the country, anywhere. You'll have more chance. Buy up a stock of supplies and get into a tent or cabin somewhere. Soon there'll be nothing but starvation in this city for such as we."

How correct Bertie Messener was, I never dreamed. I decided mentally that he was an alarmist. As for myself I was content to remain and watch the fun. After I dropped him, instead of going directly home, I went on in a hunt for more food. To my surprise, I learned that the small groceries where I had bought in the morning were sold out. I extended my search to the Potrero, and by good luck managed to pick up another box of candles, two sacks of wheat flour, ten pounds of graham flour (which would do for the servants), a case of tinned corn, and two cases of tinned tomatoes. It did look as though there was going to be at least a temporary food shortage, and I hugged myself over the goodly stock of provisions I had laid in.

The next morning I had my coffee in bed as usual, and, more than the cream, I missed the daily paper. It was this absence of knowledge of what was going on in the world that I found the chiefest hardship. Down at the club there was little news. Rider had crossed from Oakland in his launch, and Halstead had been down to San Jose and back in his machine. They reported the same condition in those places as in San Francisco. Everything was tied up by the strike. All grocery stocks had been bought out by the upper classes. And perfect order reigned. But what was happening over the rest of the country—in Chicago? New York? Washington? Most probably the same things that were happening with us, we concluded; but the fact that we did not know with absolute surety was irritating.

General Folsom had a bit of news. An attempt had been made to place army telegraphers in the telegraph offices, but the wires had been cut in every direction. This was, so far, the one unlawful act committed by labor, and that it was a concerted act he was fully convinced. He had communicated by wireless with the army post at Benicia, the telegraph lines were even then being patrolled by soldiers all the way to Sacramento. Once, for one short instant, they had got the Sacramento call, then the wires, somewhere, were cut again. General Folsom reasoned that similar attempts to open communication were being made by the authorities all the way across the continent, but he was non-committal as to whether or not he thought the attempt would succeed. What worried him was the wire-cutting; he could not but believe that it was an important part of the deep-laid labor conspiracy. Also, he regretted that the government had not long since established its projected chain of wireless stations.

The days came and went, and for a time it was a humdrum time. Nothing happened. The edge of excitement had become blunted. The streets were not so crowded. The working class did not come up town any more to see how we were taking the strike. And there were not so many automobiles running around. The repair shops and garages were closed, and whenever a machine broke down it went out of commission. The clutch on mine broke, and love nor money could not get it repaired. Like the rest, I now was walking. San Francisco lay dead, and we did not know what was happening over the rest of the country. But from the very fact that we did not know we could conclude only that the rest of the country lay as dead as San Francisco. From time to time the city was placarded with the proclamations of organized labor—these had been printed months before and evidenced how thoroughly the I. L. W. had prepared for the strike. Every detail had been worked out long in advance. No violence had occurred as yet, with the exception of the shooting of a few wire-cutters by the soldiers, but the people of the slums were starving and growing ominously restless.

The business men, the millionaires, and the professional class held meetings and passed proclamations, but there was no way of making the proclamations public. They could not even get them printed. One result of these meetings however, was that General Folsom was persuaded into taking military possession of the wholesale houses and of all the flour, grain and food warehouses. It was high time, for suffering was becoming acute in the homes of the rich, and breadlines were necessary. I know that my servants were beginning to draw long faces, and it was amazing—the hole they made in my stock of provisions. In fact, as I afterward surmised, each servant was stealing from me and secreting a private stock of provisions for himself.

But with the formation of the bread lines came new troubles. There was only so much of a food reserve in San Francisco, and at the best it could not last long. Organized labor, we knew, had its private supplies; nevertheless, the whole working class joined the bread lines. As a result, the provisions General Folsom had taken possession of diminished with perilous rapidity. How were the soldiers going to distinguish between a shabby middle-class man, a member of the I. L. W., or a slum-dweller? The first and the last had to be fed, but the soldiers did not know all the I. L. W. men in the city, much less the wives and sons and daughters of the I. L. W. men. The employers helping, a few of the known union men were flung out of the bread-lines; but that amounted to nothing. To make matters worse, the government tugs that had been hauling food from the army depots on Mare Island to Angel Island found no more food to haul. The soldiers now received their rations from the confiscated provisions, and they received them first.

The beginning of the end was in sight. Violence was beginning to show its awful face. Law and order were passing away, and passing away, I must confess, among the slum people and the upper classes. Organized labor still maintained perfect order. It could well afford to—it had plenty to eat. I remember the afternoon at the Club when I caught Halstead and Brentwood whispering in a corner. They took me in on the venture. Brentwood's machine was still in running order, and they were going out cow-stealing. Halstead had a long butcher-knife and a cleaver. We went out to the outskirts of the city. Here and there were cows grazing, but always guarded by their owners. We pursued our quest, following along the fringe of the city to the east, and on the hills near Hunter's Point we came upon a cow guarded by a little girl. There was also a young calf with the cow. We wasted no time on preliminaries. The little girl ran away screaming, while we slaughtered the cow. I omit the details, for they are not nice—we were unaccustomed to such work, and we bungled it.

But in the midst of it, working with the haste of fear, we heard cries, and we saw a number of men running toward us. We abandoned the spoils and took to our heels. To our surprise we were not pursued. Looking back, we saw the men hurriedly cutting up the cow. They had been on the same lay as ourselves. We argued that there was plenty for all, and ran back. The scene that followed beggars description. We fought and squabbled over the division like savages. Brentwood, I remember, was a perfect brute, snarling and snapping and threatening that murder would be done if we did not get our proper share.

And we were getting our share when there occurred a new irruption on the scene. This time it was the dreaded peace officers of the I. L. W. The little girl had brought them.

They were armed with whips and clubs, and there were a score of them. The little girl danced up and down in anger, the tears streaming down her cheeks, crying, "Give it to 'em! Give it to 'em! That guy with the specs— he did it! Mash his face for him! Mash his face!" That guy with the specs was I and I got my face mashed, too, though I had the presence of mind to take off my glasses at the first. My! but we did receive a trouncing as we scattered in all directions. Brentwood, Halstead and I flew away for the machine. Brentwood's nose was bleeding, while Halstead's cheek was cut across with the scarlet slash of a blacksnake whip.

And lo, when the pursuit ceased and we had gained the machine, there hiding behind it, was the frightened calf. Brentwood warned us to be cautious, and crept up on it like a wolf or tiger. Knife and cleaver had been left behind, but Brentwood still had his hands, and over and over on the ground he rolled with the poor little calf as he throttled it. We threw the carcass into the machine, covered it over with a robe, and started home. But our misfortunes had only begun. We blew out a tire.

There was no way of fixing it, and twilight was coming on. We abandoned the machine, Brentwood puffing and staggering along in advance, the calf, covered by the robe, slung across his shoulders. We took turn about carrying that calf, and it nearly killed us. Also we lost our way. And then, after hours of wandering and toil, we encountered a gang of hoodlums. They were not I. L. W. men and I guess they were as hungry as we. At any rate, they got the calf and we got the thrashing. Brentwood raged like a madman the rest of the way home, and he looked like one, what of his torn clothes, swollen nose, and blackened eyes.

There wasn't any more cow-stealing after that. General Folsom sent his troops out and confiscated all the cows, and his troopers, aided by the militia, ate most of the meat. General Folsom was not to be blamed; it was his duty to maintain law and order, and he maintained it by means of the soldiers, wherefore he was compelled to feed them first of all.

It was about this time that the great panic

occurred. The wealthy classes precipitated the flight, and then the slum people caught the contagion and stampeded wildly out of the city. General Folsom was pleased. It was estimated that at least 200,000 had deserted San Francisco, and by that much was his food problem solved. Well do I remember that day. In the morning I had eaten a crust of bread. Half of the afternoon I had stood in the bread-line; and after dark I returned home, tired and miserable, carrying a quart of rice and a slice of bacon. Brown met me at the door. His face was worn and terrified. All the servants had fled, he informed me. He alone remained. I was touched by his faithfulness, and when I learned that he had eaten nothing all day, I divided my food with him. We cooked half the rice and half the bacon, sharing it equally and reserving the other half for morning. I went to bed with my hunger, and tossed restlessly all night. In the morning I found Brown had deserted me, and, greater misfortune still, he had stolen what remained of the rice and bacon.

It was a gloomy handful of men that came together at the Club that morning. There was

no service at all. The last servant was gone.
I noticed, too, that the silver was gone, and
learned where it had gone. The servants had
not taken it, for the reason, I presume, that
the club members got it first. Their method
of disposing of it was simple. Down south of
Market street, in the dwellings of the I. L. W.,
the housewives had given square meals in ex-
change for it. I went back to my house. Yes,
my silver was gone all but a massive pitcher.
This I wrapped up and carried down south of
Market.

I felt better after the meal, and returned
to the Club to learn if there was anything new
in the situation. Hanover, Collins and Dakon
were just leaving. There was no one inside,
they told me, and they invited me to come along
with them. They were leaving the city, they
said, on Dakon's horses, and there was a spare
one for me. Dakon had four magnificent carriage horses that he wanted to save, and General Folsom had given him the tip that next
morning all the horses that remained in the
city were to be confiscated for food. There
were not many horses left, for tens of thou-

sands of them had been turned loose into the country when the hay and grain gave out during the first days. Birdall, I remember, who had great draying interests had turned loose 300 dray horses. At an average value of five hundred dollars this had amounted to $150,000. He had hoped, at first, to recover most of the horses after the strike was over, but in the end he never recovered one of them. They were all eaten by the people that fled from San Francisco. For that matter the killing of the army mules and horses for food had already begun.

Fortunately for Dakon, he had had a plentiful supply of hay and grain stored in his stable. We managed to raise four saddles, and we found the animals in good condition and spirited, withal unused to being ridden. I remembered the San Francisco of the Great Earthquake as we rode through the streets, but this San Francisco was vastly more pitiable. No cataclysm of nature had caused this, but rather the tyranny of the labor unions. We rode down past Union Square and through the theater, hotel and shopping districts. The streets were deserted. Here and there stood automobiles, abandoned where they had broken down or when the gasoline had given out. There was no sign of life, save for the occasional policeman and the soldiers, guarding the banks and public buildings. Once we came upon an I. L. W. man pasting up the latest proclamation. We stopped to read. "We have maintained an orderly strike," it ran; "and we shall maintain order to the end. The end will come when our demands are satisfied, and our demands will be satisfied when we have starved our employers into submission, as we ourselves in the past have often been starved into submission."

"Messener's very words, "Collins said. "And I, for one, am ready to submit, only they won't give me a chance to submit. I haven't had a full meal in an age. I wonder what horse-meat tastes like."

We stopped to read another proclamation: "When we think our employers are ready to submit, we shall open up the telegraphs and place the employers' associations of the United States in communication. But only messages relating to peace terms shall be permitted over the wires."

We rode on, crossed Market street, and a little later were passing through the working class districts. Here the streets were not deserted. Leaning over gates or standing in groups, were the I. L. W. men. Happy, wellfed children were playing games, and stout housewives sat on the front steps gossiping. One and all cast amused glances at us. Little children ran after us crying: "Hey, mister, ain't you hungry?" And one woman, a nursing child at her breast, called at Dakon. "Say, Fattey, I will give you a square meal for your skate—ham and potatoes, currant jelly, white bread, canned butter, and two cups of coffee."

"Have you noticed, the last few days," Hanover remarked to me, "that there's not been a stray dog in the streets?"

I had noticed, but I had not thought about it before. It was high time to leave the unfortunate city. We at last managed to connect with the San Bruno Road, along which we headed south. I had a country place near Menlo, and it was our objective. But soon we began to discover that the country was worse off and far more dangerous than the city. There, the soldiers and the I. L. W. kept order;

but the country had been turned over to anarchy. Two hundred thousand people had fled
south from San Francisco, and we had count-
less evidences that their flight had been like
fighting. Here and there we passed bodies
that of an army of locusts. They had swept
everything clean. There had been robbery and
by the roadside and saw the blackened ruins
of farmhouses. The fences were down, and the
crops had been trampled by the feet of a mul-
titude. All the vegetable patches had been
rooted up by the famished hordes. All the
chickens and farm animals had been slaughtered. This was true of all the main roads
that led out of San Francisco. Here and there,
away from the roads, farmers had held their
own with shotguns and revolvers, and were
still holding their own. They warned us away
and refused to parley with us. And all the
destruction and violence had been done by the
slum-dwellers and the upper classes. The I. L.
W. men, with plentiful food supplies, remained
quietly in their homes in the cities.

Early in the day we received concrete proof
of how desperate was the situation. To the

right of us we heard cries and rifle shots. Bullets whistled dangerously near. There was a crashing in the underbrush; then a magnificent black truck-horse broke across the road in front of us and was gone. We had barely time to notice that he was bleeding and lame. He was followed by three soldiers. The chase went on amongst the trees on the left. We could hear the soldiers calling to one another. A fourth soldier limped out upon the road from the right, sat down on a boulder, and mopped the sweat from his face.

The man grinned up at us and asked for a match. In reply to Dakon's "What's the word?" he informed us that the militiamen were deserting. "No grub," he exclaimed. "They're feedin' it all to the regulars." We also learned from him that the military prisoners had been released from Alcatraz Island because they could no longer be fed.

I shall never forget the next sight we encountered. We came upon it abruptly, around a turn of the road. Overhead arched the trees. The sunshine was fiiltering down through the branches. Butterflies were fluttering by, and from the fields came the song of larks. And there it stood a powerful touring car. About it and in it lay a number of corpses. It told its own tale. Its occupants, fleeing from the city, had been attacked and dragged down by a gang of slum-dwellers—hoodlums. The thing had occurred within twenty-four hours. Freshly opened meat and fruit tins explained the reason for the attack. Dakon examined the bodies.

"I thought so," he reported. "I've ridden in that car. It was Periton—the whole family. We've got to watch out for ourselves from now on."

"But we had no food with which to invite attack," I objected.

Dakon pointed to the horse I rode, and I understood.

Early in the day Dakon's horse had cast a shoe. The delicate hoof had split, and by noon the animal was limping. Dakon refused to ride it further, and refused to desert it. So, on his solicitation, we went on. He would lead the horse and join us at my place. That was the last we saw of him; nor did we ever learn his end.

By one o'clock we arrived at the town of

Menlo, or rather at the site of Menlo, for it was in ruins. Corpses lay everywhere. The business part of the town, as well as part of the residences, had been gutted by fire. Here and there a residence still held out; but there was no getting near them. When we approached too closely we were fired upon. We met a woman who was poking about in the smoking ruins of her cottage. The first attack, she told us, had been on the stores, and as she talked we could picture that raging, roaring, hungry mob flinging itself upon the handful of townspeople. Millionaires and paupers had fought side by side for the food, and then fought with one another after they got it. The town of Palo Alto and Sanford University had been sacked in similar fashion, we learned. Ahead of us lay a desolate wasted land; and we thought we were wise in turning off to my place. It lay three miles to the west, snuggling among the first rolling swells of the foothills.

But as we rode along we saw that the devastation was not confined to the main roads. The van of the flight had kept to the roads, sacking the small towns as it went; while those that followed had scattered out and swept the whole countryside like a great broom. My place was built of concrete, masory, and tiles and so had escaped being burned, but it was gutted clean. We found the gardener's body in the windmill, littered around with empty shotgun shells. He had put up a good fight. But no trace could be found of the two Italian laborers, nor of the housekeeper and her husband. Not a living thing remained. The calves, the colts, all the fancy poultry and thoroughbred stock, everything was gone. The kitchen and the fireplace where the mob had cooked, were a mess, while many campfires outside bore witness to the large number that had fed and spent the night. What they had not eaten they had carried away. There was not a bite for us.

We spent the rest of the night vainly waiting for Dakon, and in the morning, with our revolvers, fought off half a dozen marauders. Then we killed one of Dakon's horses, hiding for the future what meat we did not immediately eat. In the afternoon Collins went out for a walk, but failed to return. This was the last straw to Hanover. He was for flight there and then, and I had great difficulty in persuading him to wait for daylight. As for myself, I was convinced that the end of the general strike was near, and I was resolved to return to San Francisco. So, in the morning we parted company, Hanover heading south, fifty pounds of horse meat ·strapped to his saddle, while I, similarly loaded, headed north. Little Hanover pulled through all right, and to the end of his life he will persist, I know, in boring everybody with the narrative of his subsequent adventures.

I got as far as Belmont, on the main road back, when I was robbed of my horse-meat by three militiamen. There was no change in the situation, they said, except that it was going from bad to worse. The I. L. W. had plenty of provisions hidden away and could last out for months. I managed to get as far as Baden, when my horse was taken away from me by a dozen men. Two of them were San Francisco policemen, and the remainder were regular soldiers. This was ominous. The situation was certainly extreme when the regulars were beginning to desert. When I continued my way on foot, they already had the fire started, and the last of Dakon's horses lay slaughtered on the ground.

As luck would have it, I sprained my ankle, and succeeded in getting no further than South San Francisco. I lay there that night in an outhouse, shivering with the cold and at the same time burning with fever. Two days I lay there, too sick to move, and on the third, reeling and giddy, supporting myself on an extemporized crutch I tottered on toward San Francisco. I was weak as well, for it was the third day since food had passed my lips. It was a day of nightmare and torment. As in a dream I passed hundreds of regular soldiers drifting along in the opposite direction, and many policemen, with their families, organized in large groups for mutual protection.

As I entered the city I remembered the workman's house at which I had traded the silver pitcher, and in that direction my hunger drove me. Twilight was falling when I came to the place. I passed around by the alleyway and crawled up the back steps, on which I collapsed. I managed to reach out with the crutch and knocked at the door. Then I must have fainted, for I came to in the kitchen, my face wet with water and whisky being poured down my throat. I choked and spluttered and tried to talk; I began by saying something about not having any more silver pitchers, but that I would make it up to them afterward if they would only give me something to eat. But the housewife interrupted me.

"Why, you poor man!" she said. "Haven't you heard? The strike was called off this afternoon. Of course we'll give you something to eat."

She hustled around, opening a tin of breakfast bacon and preparing to fry it.

"Let me have some now, please," I begged; and I ate the raw bacon on a slice of bread, while her husband explained that the demands of the I. L. W. had been granted. The wires had been opened up in the early afternoon, and everywhere the employers' association had given in. There hadn't been any employers left in San Francisco, but General Folsom had spoken for them. The trains and steamers would start running in the morning, and so would everything else just as soon as system could be established.

And that was the end of the general strike. I never want to see another one. It was worse than a war. A general strike is a cruel and immoral thing, and the brain of man should be capable of running industry in a more rational way. Harrison is still my chauffeur. It was part of the conditions of the I. L. W. that all of its members should be reinstated in their old positions. Brown never came back, but the rest of the servants are with me. I hadn't the heart to discharge them—poor creatures, they were pretty hard pressed when they deserted with the food and silver. And now I can't discharge them. They have all been unionized by the I. L. W. The tyranny of organized labor is getting beyond human endurance. Something must be done.

Other Titles in Pocket Series

Fiction

History, Biography

Humor

Literature

Maxims and Epigrams

Philosophy, Religion

Series of Debates

Miscellaneous